ON
PRAYER

ON
PRAYER

A Letter to My Godchild

PHYLLIS ZAGANO

Liguori
LIGUORI, MISSOURI

Published by Liguori Publications
Liguori, Missouri
www.liguori.org
www.catholicbooksonline.com

Originally published as *On Prayer* in 1994 by Paulist Press, Mahwah, New Jersey.

Library of Congress Cataloging-in-Publication Data

Zagano, Phyllis.
      On prayer : a letter to my godchild / Phyllis Zagano.
            p.   cm.
      Originally published: Mahwah, N.J. : Paulist Press, 1994.
      ISBN 0-7648-0795-1 (pbk.)
      1. Spiritual life—Catholic Church. 2. Prayer—Catholic Church.
I. Title.

BX2350.3 .Z34 2001
248.3'2—dc21   2001036684

Printed in the United States of America
05 04 03 02 01   5 4 3 2 1
Revised edition 2001

FOR M.G.

Acknowledgments

The publisher gratefully acknowledges use of the following materials: Scripture passages from *The New Jerusalem Bible,* copyright © 1985, by Doubleday, a Division of Bantam Doubleday Dell Publishing Group, Inc. Reprinted by permission: selections from *The Grail Psalms,* copyright © 1963, 1986 by Ladies of the Grail (England), used by permission of GIA Publications, Inc., Chicago, Illinois, exclusive agent. All rights reserved. Psalms from *The Liturgy of the Hours,* Catholic Book Publishing Co., New York, 1976.

Contents

CONTENTS

Preface to the Second Edition

S ometimes things take on a life of their own. This book, for example, came about because I promised my godchild a book on prayer. Not that I was going to write one. I only promised to buy one. But the books I found at the time, in a very respectable but now closed religious bookstore in Manhattan, were either too technical or too frothy. I was looking for simplicity and reality, because I truly believe that simplicity and reality are the basics and the basis of holiness.

At the time I was focusing on people who were around the age of my godchild and of my students at the university. That they deserve to hear about holiness in simple and direct language is a given. Giving them what they deserve turned out to be a bit harder. So, when I could not find a book that I thought suited their need, I sat down to write one.

Not that that was any easier.

I had been teaching at a university for about twenty years by then, and had helped out at various campus ministries along the way. So I turned to my teaching assistant, a young woman, and other young people from the campus Newman Center for assistance. They helped by reading the manuscript as I went along, taking four or five pages at a time, and coming back with questions that would guide the next four or five pages, and so on. Finally, my friend Mary Sweeney, SC, a campus minister, read the manuscript completely, and suggested some of the Scripture passages at its end. Other friends, especially Carolyn O'Hara, OCD, and Irene Kelly, RSHM, took a look at my work-in-progress.

The head of the university Newman Center, a Paulist priest named Father Jim Donovan, suggested I send the manuscript to his friend, Father Kevin Lynch, CP, which I did. A short time later a Paulist editor, Dennis McManus, telephoned to say they were accepting the manuscript. My working title for the book, *For My Godchild, On Prayer*, was changed to simply *On Prayer,* and the book found many admirers from around the world. It has been translated into Italian, and may be translated some day into Spanish and the Indonesian languages. Along the way, I have been somewhat surprised to hear from older people—at least those older than my twenty-one-year-old godchild and my twenty-something university students—who have found the book helpful. I particularly recall a conversation with a middle-aged woman religious, who said she was encouraged by my saying, right there in public, that sometimes you have to learn to pray all over again, and sometimes more than once.

Of course that is true. I think as we journey in the spiritual life we truly do get waylaid or offtrack or just forget what it was we started out to do. And so we begin again. That is OK. There is nothing worse than thinking that this particular terribly intimate part of our lives is closed to future development, that this chapter is ended never to be taken up again. God is always there, waiting for us to look around and recognize his presence. And God will grant whatever gifts we need to get moving, to get back on track, to remember what it is all about.

I had someone else tell me she was above all this simple stuff, that she wanted something more complex; at her age (about eighty) she thought she knew all the basics. I have thought about that many times. Yes, there are technical explanations of what happens in prayer, especially in mystical-contemplative prayer. But I don't think most people are mystics. I touch on mysticism in this little book, but I don't want to get off the mark by trying to convince the reader that there is some sort of goal in prayer, because there really isn't, beyond giving up your will—inside and out—to God.

I spent many years at Boston University, with my principal appointment in the College of Communication and minor appointments in the School of Theology and the College of Liberal Arts (International Relations). I specialized in the social impact of mass media, and on religion and media. I published a lot. I had a radio program on the National Public Radio affiliate. Just before writing this book, I became Faculty-in-Residence as well. Neither this book about prayer, nor my book *Woman to Woman: An Anthology of Women's Spiritualities* was well received by my colleagues. In fact, my chairman told me that the department did not wish to be affiliated with "that sort of thing." I've been told I was "too Catholic" before. No sense fighting it. It is the last acceptable prejudice.

So I stopped talking about mass media, and denominational statements, and political theory to write yet another book, *Holy Saturday: An Argument for the Restoration of the Female Diaconate in the Catholic Church* (Crossroad/Herder, 2000).

Which is exactly the point.

MARCH 25, 2001
NEW YORK CITY

Preface

At about midnight at my godchild's twenty-first birthday party, the two of us sat at the kitchen table and talked about God and church and religion and prayer. We live quite far apart and do not see each other all that often so I wanted to slip one last godmotherly conversation in under the adulthood deadline. That is how this very private little book came to be, and I am grateful to my godchild for allowing me to share it with you.

SEPTEMBER 21, 1993
FEAST OF ST. MATTHEW
NEW YORK CITY

On Prayer

Here is what I promised you at your birthday party. Talking about prayer is probably one of the hardest things I can think of doing, as well as one of the easiest. I am not sure I know anything about prayer, except that without it I think I would fall down. With prayer I know that God's hand is ever at my back, guiding me, consoling me, sometimes holding me back, sometimes holding me up. Without that hand, without prayer, I am quite sure I might fall down. To me, prayer means talking and being with God, and God talking and being with me.

I know you have an understanding of God, and of what it means to pray. You may even have seen one of the many manuals that present instruction on prayer. This is not an instruction book. It is more my prayer for you. These few words are what I have learned about prayer and about praying, mostly since the day I held you in the church twenty-one years ago and we declared you Christian. Since I participated in that deci-

1

sion on your behalf, before I leave you to your own devices I ought to tell you all, or at least most, of what little I know about the very positive and beautiful experience of prayer.

So I hope and pray these next few pages will help you to understand what it is that is going on inside you. I also hope that what follows here will help you make the effort to keep up the relationship you already have with God. I want you to pray, and as your Godmother I have the right to want that for you. I want you to know God and to nurture that knowledge. I want you to love him in your own right, not because someone has told you it is the acceptable thing to do, but because you have grown to know and to love him on your own. Knowing and loving God, and making him known and loved, are the most important things in my own life, so you can appreciate my prejudice in your behalf. Take what I say, if you will, and consider it at least as the wish I have for you as you begin your adult life, alone, in the care of the God whom I have asked to protect you for every day of each of these past twenty-one years.

Praying

Praying is as simple as breathing. In fact, some spiritual writers tell us that the way to keep in touch with that magnificent reality we know as God is to "breathe" a word or phrase as we go along our daily business. Some people use a small word or phrase—like "Jesus" or "my Lord"—and repeat it endlessly as they go about their daily tasks. This is, of course, often impossible as you struggle with your university studies. But there are moments when you can recall that you live and breathe in God's presence, that he cares for you with a mighty care, as great and as deep as that of your parents and me, and then greater still, and deeper. Some people use a longer phrase, perhaps attuned to their walking stride, such as "Lord Jesus, Son of the living God, have mercy on me a sinner." I don't know if that would work as a rhythm for you while you row in crew; I know it works fine for me when I walk or run.

The purpose of this kind of exercise may seem a

little indistinct for you now, but, believe me, it is important. The biggest, and I mean the biggest, trap anyone faces in a life of prayer—and this goes for all of us, at twenty-one or forty-five or eighty—is ourselves. What I mean is, we are really very fond of ourselves, whether we admit it or not, and the biggest trap in your prayer life is yourself. It is, after all, much more interesting to have an agreeable and admiring audience. So, instead of praying, many times we fall into the convenience of merely talking to ourselves. Talking to yourself is something everybody does—but it is important not to do it too much or too often, especially when you are trying to pray. At its simplest, praying means talking to someone else, and that someone else is the God who not only made you, but who redeemed you and who sustains your every breath.

In essence, the prayerful person is in constant conversation with the God he or she knows and loves. To know and love God is why you were made. This is a curious fact, since loving God and knowing God does not change God in the least. But it changes us, and changes us powerfully. As God's wonderful creations, we come to recognize that loving him helps us know he has loved us into being, into our very existence, and that he continues to do so. It also teaches us that his love cannot be contained.

Inevitably, if we know and love God through prayer we find that we must go out of ourselves, we must leave this wonderful relationship, to extend God's love to others in service. This does not mean you need to tell the parish priest to retire, at least not yet. Not everyone is called to a professional life of prayer and service, but everyone is most assuredly called to a personal life of prayer and service, if only insofar as our prayer has made us calmer, kinder, and a bit nicer toward those around us, especially those in need.

This is another effect of real prayer. If we are genuinely praying, we cannot help but be concerned with others—so much so that we are willing to sacrifice the time we have set aside for prayer in order to help them, or calm them, or listen to their troubles. There is another trap here, because the prayer which drives us to help them is the prayer which nourishes our ability to help. As with everything else, we need to strike a balance. Of course your own common sense tells you that it is both foolish and rude to turn away someone in need just because your appointed time for prayer has come. The person who will not listen to another in order to engage in personal prayer is perhaps not aware that simply looking reverently at the person in need is reverencing the Christ he says he loves so well. There is often nothing we can do when someone comes before us broken except to look at him or her and recognize the Christ. We must listen to this broken Christ before us and hear how someone else has not seen that same beauty, has not realized that to deal with another person—this very person—is to deal with Christ. This person when broken, no matter what his or her actual position in life, is in fact the homeless, is in fact the voiceless, is in fact the powerless we claim to care so much about. Just listening reverently to the broken one before us is as great a prayer (as well as a lesson in our own powerlessness) as we can ever achieve.

Of course the opposite is also true. By that I mean that we can often get so caught up in good works, in doing things for other people, that we begin to think that we are doing something to help them, and that we are somehow not only instruments of God's providence but direct contact agents of his will. This is when you need to watch out that you don't fall over your own ego, because there is really nothing any of us can do except to cooperate with God's will, however it may unfold. Therefore, to think we can change God's will is a little foolhardy, and can hurt us just as much as it can hurt the person whose life we have decided to redirect. It is a wonderful temptation to run another person's life, and the thing we need to learn when praying for and praying with another is to stand back and simply reverence him or her, and let the Lord's word and work unfold as beautifully in the other as it can unfold in us. I think that may be why you are so upset about the Church these days. There are plenty of "Mr. Fix-its" around, and sometimes they do not have the time (or at least do not think they have the time) to listen to the word of God as it works in your life, in God's time and not in theirs. That is why it is important for you to work at, and I mean really work at, your own relationship with God, because as you do you will begin to notice what comes from God, and what comes from you, and what comes from a force outside you that is both hopeless and definitively opposed to your life with God. Not that the helpful others are coming from evil, not at all. It is just that sometimes people in their haste to do good lay us open to a weakness that lets in the bad, and we are all confused and then even more prey to what is not from God, because it seems so easy and so comfortable at first.

Let me explain. Suppose you know in your heart that it is right to visit a sick relative, or spend time helping your mother. Someone might encourage you to "live your own life" or "spend some time on yourself" without understanding that you do live your own life and spend plenty of time on yourself. If you listen to them instead of to yourself, in the light of God's word, you might move away from what you know to be right. That is a minor move, but minor moves become major after a while.

I wonder if I sound as if I am getting off the topic. I think not. The single most important way for you to know right from wrong, and especially the right for your life from the wrong for your life, is to nurture a relationship with God. He loves you, I promise you that, and he will care for you in ways I cannot describe, because they are so deep, so personal, and so loving, and because they defy analogy or explanation. And just as it is hopelessly rude to ignore the person who stands before you in need, it is similarly hopelessly rude to ignore yourself and your own needs. This is especially true of your need to be alone with God for whatever part of the day you find really necessary. Prayer takes time, a lot of time. The time you spend is genuinely squandered, like the ointment poured out on Jesus' feet. The paradox is that it is the very squandering of time that prepares you so well for the future, for the gifts of peace, of consolation, of a genuine self-understanding; what seems like time wasted is really time spent getting to know this tremendous lover. You know what it means to "waste" time walking on the beach with a friend. I encourage you to "waste" time with God in the very same way.

God

All of this presupposes your acknowledging a need to be alone with God, and a willingness to leave your defenses, leave what defines you externally, and leave your very will aside to encounter this magnificent other.

To a certain extent, praying presupposes that you have a God whom you know. Yet it is in the very act of praying that you learn to know him. Who is this God, anyway? We all talk a great deal about God, and we assume we and everyone else know whom we are talking about, but I think you will find that the most difficult question anyone could ever ask of you is: "Who is God?" This, of course, is the objective, the scientific way of asking. So you would likely answer as I do: Creator, Redeemer, Sanctifier; Father, Son, and Spirit. The God revealed in Scripture, as explained by Jesus, is the God in whom I believe.

But there is a deeper question, more aptly put: "Who is *your* God?" or "Who is it that you love?" or

"Who is the God you pray to?" I cannot tell you the answer to this question. Some people call God their best friend, or their significant other, or the Wholly Other, or their lover. All of these terms are inadequate, and never really catch the personal experience of God; at best they are mere analogies to what you experience when you are really involved with God. For example, when you talk with God about something very troubling, God can be closer than your best friend or your mother because you probably find you are not embarrassed, or at least not that embarrassed, when you talk about such matters. There are many, many things we cannot bear to reveal to even those closest to us, yet God can be the one you turn to where otherwise you might be too humiliated or too fearful to turn to anyone else.

What God says or seems to say to you at these times deserves examination, because there are a number of things that can happen. I had a professor of moral theology who called his response to confusion "the grandmother theory." Basically, if what God seems to say to you would make sense to a grandmother, it is probably OK. Not *your* grandmother, you understand, just *a* grandmother who can hear the case objectively and render a decision. This is important because we often feel that something is good for us when in fact it is not.

Prayer involves feelings as well as thoughts and words, and it is with feelings that we recognize the validity of the thoughts and words that seem to come to us. Here, in the realm of feeling, you need to examine very carefully what is going on because, as I said, there are essentially three possibilities: you might be talking with yourself, with God, or with evil.

I would not be terribly afraid here, but you are as good a target for the devil as anyone else. And anyone who says the devil, as the name of the negative force of evil opposed to what we know of as the good, does not exist is kidding himself. There are many tricks that evil plays on us, especially as we begin to try to talk with God, either for the first time or for one of the many times we find we need to begin again. One trick is to convince us that there is no devil, no negative force, that seeks to drain the life of God from the world. Another is to convince us that it is OK to spend a lot of time talking with ourselves instead of with God, or that talking with ourselves is really prayer. It is not. But since talking with ourselves is a very comfortable way to think about our joys and sorrows, and it feels good, we do not mind just a little bit of self-indulgence, because we believe it is useful. It is not. Certain types of self-involvement, such as intellectual work, or logical and factual introspection relative to a decision, are good and healthy. But the time we set aside for prayer is not time for these. The time we set aside for prayer must be used for prayer, or not at all. I hate to sound like a strict schoolteacher about this, but it is very important not to confuse the two. The times we set aside for prayer can be times of open and honest relaxation in the arms of God, and nothing else. Here is where we work, sometimes painfully, at this most wonderful relationship. If we start to let other concerns eat away at this time, we will find that we have not been praying at all, day after day, and year after year. This often results in a very dangerous, and essentially self-centered, way of being.

So it is important at the outset to determine what it feels like for you to be in the presence of God, and for you to be talking with God. If you think back over the years, you will recall times when you just "knew" you were praying. You just "knew" you were involved with God. Somehow there was a closeness, a peace, a simplicity, and an evenness to your feelings that let you know that God was there, present to you. Perhaps this came at a time of reconciliation, when something that weighed heavily on your mind was finally gotten rid of, and you celebrated that fact with a representative of the Church. Or perhaps, once, at the communion of a Mass, you found yourself folded into the warmth of the music and the candlelight in a peaceful security that you just cannot quite put your finger on, nor can you bring it about yourself. Or perhaps you sat, alone, in a church, not particularly saying anything to God, or even God saying anything in particular to you, and yet you knew a depth to your person and your personality that, when you think back on it, is extraordinarily powerful and real even now. These may be examples of the peace of God's presence, and as you test and retest yourself over the years, you will begin to recognize immediately when you have been drawn into a deep communion with God. In fact, after a while you may find that there is just nothing to say at these times. You simply look at him, and he looks at you, and you know a beautiful and deep acceptance and love of your entire being, because the one you know as your Creator, your Redeemer, your Sanctifier, loves you as his own.

Adoration

There is something very beautiful about just looking at God and letting him look at you, in knowing how accepted you are by him, and how his acceptance encourages you to accept yourself, warts and all, as a beautiful creation of God's love. Spiritual writers divide what we do in prayer into four categories: adoration (or praise), contrition, petition, and thanksgiving. These are the four basic movements of the heart, and most of what we do in prayer falls into one or another of them, sometimes two or three, many times all.

Adoration means exactly what it sounds like. You, I am sure, know how it feels to just look at someone you love. Just being in the same room with this person is calming and reassuring; gazing at him or her in love makes you feel like a deep and still pool of cool water, undisturbed, unplumbed, unbelievably deep and alive. This also happens when we look at God.

People talk in many different ways about this movement of prayer as a special kind of prayer. In some ways of talking about it, there is an emphasis on self-awareness. In order to concentrate on the one we love, we still our senses and our minds, and concentrate on the beauty of the other. Centering prayer, as this kind of prayer is known, helps us to concentrate on the fact of our being, and eventually leads us into an understanding of ourselves as creatures, wholly dependent upon God. The phenomenon of centering prayer is such that we find ourselves very, very peaceful when we practice it regularly.

The trap of centering prayer, like the trap of any other kind of prayer, is that we begin to prefer the peacefulness to the engagement with others, even with God, the Wholly Other, and we control our thoughts and inner movements so that the peace is not disturbed, even by the Lord. Despite this danger, it is very important to learn to center our lives in prayer. We simply must remember to center our lives, in prayer, on God. There are other disciplines that use the techniques of centering prayer, where "meditation" is the goal and the end. However salutary this may be for inner peace and harmony with one's life, it is not prayer unless it is directed at the praise and adoration and actual knowing of the God whom you have grown to know and love.

I admit my prejudice in this matter because my

God is the God I have learned about from Jesus and the apostles through Scripture. So, when I am privileged to be silent in praise and adoration before God, I honor him as the Wholly Other, not the wholly opposite. I know God as a being totally distinct from my being and my realm of possibility, yet whose qualities I see reflected in myself and in the world around me. Hence, I marvel at the totality of God's goodness, gentleness, compassion, might, joy, peace, completeness, understanding, gracefulness, openness, intelligence, beauty, majesty, and the totality of his love for me. Just as I looked at you as an infant in my arms, and you looked at me, both of us in simple and loving acceptance, so God looks at me, and I at him. There is a wonderment of words to describe God in praise and adoration, and none at all really suffices.

Again, this simplest form of prayer is the form you know well in other areas. You have, I am sure, experienced the wonder of looking at a rainbow, or a sunrise. There is nothing to do but stand, however briefly, in awe of that which is before you. So it is with God, who can and will similarly capture you if you allow him to.

The words people use to categorize prayer are often confusing. In a way, what I am talking about here can be called contemplation. Some people will tell you I should finish with contemplation, not start with it, because it is the "highest" type of prayer. That may be true, but it is highest because it is simplest and purest. I just don't see the need to withhold telling you about the basic and natural response we all have to God, or to complicate it with all manner of instructions, half of which you would not recall anyway.

The practice of being sensitive to the presence of God is the single most important thing you can teach yourself about prayer. The peace of God's presence is so deep and so sweet that you will inevitably allow yourself to be drawn into it more and more as you notice it.

But then what? Most of us are ordinary people. We know when we are in God's presence, and we reverence his life and light within ourselves as we adore his presence before us, most often in the eucharistic presence—the Blessed Sacrament. But many times that recognition of God's presence, deep as it is, is fleeting. Before we know it, it has passed. We know in our minds that we are still in God's presence, but we do not feel it in our hearts. This is where prayer becomes a learned response to the Lord's invitation to be with him in the most intimate way. It really is a habit that needs to be developed, nurtured, watched, and cared for. And, while it is not overly elusive, it can slip away from you without your even noticing until you are back to talking with yourself or your friends in your mind's eye instead of talking with God.

The easiest thing to do when the conversation has turned inward is to gently redirect it outward. If the memory of a friend has distracted you, just hold that friend up to God, and maybe even talk with God about the distraction. There is no sense fussing that you are not getting holy feelings because your friend's dilemma has come across your mind. Just ask God to care for your friend. Believe me, the feelings will take care of themselves.

Contrition

The second major category of what we do in prayer is "contrition." This is not as dreary as it might sound, for it is merely a recognition of our very nature as created beings. What we tend to trip over in life are things that, while apparently good, are really not helpful in allowing us to grow in God's love as his beloved creatures. So, if we are willing to accept that there are two types of choices we can make—choices that are creative and life-giving, and choices that are not—then we need to say something to God about the "negative choices" we have made or accepted in our lives. For some of these choices, we generally need to express contrition.

This is not the same as "going to confession," which to my mind comes after we have expressed contrition in our hearts to God and then need to celebrate that fact with a representative of the Church. Contrition is where we meet the humble Jesus, and learn how much of our human frailty he understands.

Contrition is more than saying "sorry." I think for me contrition is a recognition of my own limitations and weaknesses, combined with an understanding of my total dependence upon God as Creator, Redeemer, and Sanctifier. When we are moved to speak in prayer, many times it is in recognition of the ways in which we have failed. Of course I do not mean here the laundry list of petty sins we learned to recite in first or second grade. Even now I can recall conversations with my classmates over whether any had stolen a pencil lately, that being the principal example relative to the seventh commandment. While reviewing the commandments in the presence of God is a helpful exercise (and one that I hope you will engage in at least once per month), there is a deeper meaning to the prayer of contrition that ought naturally to spring from your heart as you move along in your life of love of God.

The kinds of questions you learn to think about in philosophy class are useful here: Who am I? Why am I here? and the like. These are the measure of your contrition your whole lifelong, because as you discover your personality and your vocation, you will grow to know that you are charged with living both fully. There will be times when you just did not measure up, you just did not respond as fully or as carefully or as honestly as you might to whatever request or challenge life has brought you, and you feel that failing as it scratches against the very tender skin of your conscience. Here is where it is important to pounce upon the fault or failing and talk with God about it, because if you let it go, even for a day, the next time it will not seem quite so bad, or quite so important, and so you will let it go again. Life's major wrong choices are merely a compilation of wrong minor choices, and to avoid these small wrong turns is to avoid a very major derailment.

One way of looking at it is to note how you have failed in the virtues which oppose the seven deadly sins: pride, envy, anger, sloth, lust, greed, and gluttony, rather than in trying to find these horrific failings in yourself. Of course, we are all a little lazy from time to time, or a little angry, or a little greedy. But the bleakness that the soul beholds when it is really captivated by these seven sins (or ways of sinfulness) is such that it takes real work to be really involved in each of them.

Even so, the corruptions of this world often appear to be their opposites, and so we find ourselves powerfully attracted by one or another of these sins at various times in our lives. To truly have and live their opposing virtues is something we can beg for, and we often beg for these virtues when engaged in the prayer of contrition. When we recognize a failing, God often prompts us to ask for the healing virtue that will restore us to completeness. So, when we have been proud, we will be prompted to ask for humility; when we have been gluttonous, for temperance; when we have been lustful, for chastity. God's grace calls us to true contrition, and his healing power can overcome even the most stubborn failing if we let it.

I think contrition is a dicey subject, because we can get so involved with minuscule recollection of our every act and motive, we can become scrupulous. This is not that helpful, and it is often well to talk with God about scrupulosity, because it so often spills into other areas of our lives and can turn us into hypercritical bores. So, while it is good to be very, very sensitive to the problem areas of our lives, it is not good to be such a careful housecleaner that you are depressed all the time at how awful you are. This is, in fact, a form of pride. For what are you doing but calling yourself the all-county champion sinner in your age and class?

We are all called to live life to the fullest, and that means in large part being who you can be. Anything less probably needs an apology. Contrition often includes a deep request to God that he grant you his comfort, along with his help, in living as you ought. Without that attitude, all you are doing is setting a lot of laundry out on the line and perhaps for no particular reason other than to show it off.

Petition

I think in moving from contrition to petition it becomes useful to remember that we still need to be strengthened in God's gratuitous gifts to us: faith, hope, and charity. The theologians call these the theological virtues, but no one needs a degree to know that God grants each of these to us, wonderfully, lavishly, and gently. In fact, it is fair to say that after you have prayed for a while about something, you will notice that your response is growth in one of these. Again, I cannot tell you what or when or how. Perhaps you will find yourself in a desperate situation, unable to pray, because you did not get something that you were sure God promised you. If you pray, or try to pray, I promise you that God will somehow fill you with hope, even when such a feeling makes absolutely no sense in your situation at all. So it is with faith and with charity. I know this sounds miraculous, too good to be true. It is. It is miraculous. It is good. And it is true.

We can ask God to increase our faith, our hope,

our charity. These "theological virtues" are both measure and mark of our progress, as we ask for other virtues as well. I said above that when we find ourselves involved with the seven deadly sins and their relations we need to ask for their opposing virtues as the cures. The cardinal virtues, as they are called, are prudence, justice, temperance, and fortitude. We could go on forever talking about how they call us to live a moral life and help us to live a prayerful life. It might be better for you just to pray a little bit about how they apply to you, because it would be awfully presumptuous of me to think you need an increase in any one, or in one more than in another.

I can, of course, give you definitions for them. Prudence means the habit of choosing well, or rightly, in accordance with ourselves and with our circumstances; in essence it means choosing the will of God. Justice means being fair in all we do and say, not bending to our own insecurities, and doing the right thing even against popular opinion. Temperance means controlling our own natural desires, inclinations, and temperament, both interiorly and exteriorly. And fortitude means being brave in doing good, despite what fears might beset us.

These four pillars of the virtuous life have other virtues to support them, including obedience, truthfulness, patience, humility, chastity, liberality (the right use of goods), generosity, and piety. There are others we can look to, and you may come immediately upon one I have forgotten. As you read the list I am sure you understand the proper attitude toward each one, but sometimes it is good to ask God to guide you more specifically in one or the other. Each can present its quandaries when we least expect it. Take obedience. We all have to obey in certain ways. But it is hard to know sometimes whether God calls us to seemingly disobey a rightful order or if what we think is God's voice is merely our own self-will trumpeting our own beliefs.

If you pray for obedience, God will teach it to you, and will teach you the difference in any circumstance, large or small. I think I learned this best from a nine-year-old Hasidic boy in Brooklyn who had been hit and slightly injured by a car on a Saturday. As you know, Saturday is the sabbath for Jewish people, and Hasidim are very religious. His ankle was injured, possibly broken, and he could not walk. Because it was cold, some men moved him into a nearby store while the police went to get his mother. I sat down next to him, not touching him, and said that I would put my arm around him to comfort him, but I knew that as an Hasidic male he could not allow a woman to touch him. He looked up at me, crying, and said in one quick tearful burst: "It's OK, it's an emergency." As I sat with my arm around that nine-year-old I thanked God for this instruction. Obedience, after all, includes common sense and doing the right thing.

That is just one example, and I am sure you can think of others where it is possible to forget that simply doing the right thing is all we are asked to do, no matter what the circumstances. Consider patience. It is by now trite to say that patience is a virtue. We so often hear this that I wonder if we really know it, or what it can entail. Patience means much more than simply waiting for something we want, or for Christmas, or for things to just get better. Patience involves us, like anything else, with others. I know my own impatience is usually cured when I recognize that I can try to find a charitable explanation for everything everyone does. I do not mean here we have to excuse every stupid remark or act. But we can go a little easy on the ones who have tried our patience by remembering that sometimes others do not have all the information they need to make a decision, even when they think they do.

Popular magazine psychologists talk about "hostility levels" and "anger," but not about charitable explanations. I can remember hearing a very angry—and impatient—woman talk about another person essentially cutting ahead of her in the ophthalmologist's office. I listened to her recite the story. What, she bellowed, could that person have to talk about with the eye doctor that was so much more important than her appointment? The fact was, I did not know. But I suggested that since the second person was an artist, and a diabetic, and had just had eye surgery, perhaps there was a genuine immediate concern about bleeding in an eye. I was not there, I did not know, but I did not see any reason to become so outright hostile toward the artist when there might have been a perfectly reasonable explanation. The woman whose appointment had been delayed agreed.

The kinds of examples the popular writers give suffice just as well. There is no need to police the ten-item checkout line at the supermarket. It is usually easier to assume that people of good will know how to count, and people who apparently cannot count are probably of good will anyway. Patience, if we ask for it, will come. An automatic negative judgment does something to us that I cannot exactly describe, but it is not good.

God will eventually explain everything that happens to us, yet it is important for us to try as best we can to explain things to ourselves. This is why we pray to ask to understand the virtues properly. When we are talking with God about a specific incident in our lives, we must remember to ask for what we need. Sometimes we can come away from prayer and realize that we forgot to ask God to help us in one or another specific area. We just forgot to ask for what we wanted. I will not say that this is because we do not trust God, or we do not love God, or we do not believe God can grant us our deepest needs. I think we just forget. Petition is part of every prayer; it is implicit in everything we hold up to God, whether we stand before him like a child showing him a hurt finger or showing off a brand-new balloon. We are asking him to do whatever he will: kiss the finger or smile at the balloon. I think petition often means hanging around to see how God answers, and recognizing when an answer really is from him. That is the hardest part of asking for help.

So, in addition to asking to understand the virtuous life, when we pray there are other things we ask for. This third area, the prayer of "petition," is pretty familiar to most of us. Here we ask God for what we want, and ask him to guard us from what we don't want. I think I really learned about the prayer of petition on an airplane, both in the ordinary sense, and in the real sense.

By the ordinary sense I mean that we simply go

before God and tell him what we think we need. These are the aches in our souls—the fears, the needs, the wants. God, of course, knows all we need before we ask it, but there is something consoling about presenting these needs. What we are doing is simply seeing how he responds to them. The frightened plea for the airplane to please land, safely and quickly, is genuine in its dependence on God. The heartache and humiliation of unemployment, presented often and regularly during a period of real struggle, eventually leads to a deeper understanding of that same dependence. This is where the prayer of petition, in the real sense, comes into play. Asking God to keep us safe and asking God to find us employment are really the same prayer. By acknowledging our dependence on God, we may eventually give ourselves over to the notion that his will comes about in all of us, even despite our best efforts to thwart it.

What we must understand eventually about the prayer of petition is that God's plans are not ours. I know that may sound trite, but it is a very hard lesson to learn. Hence, the prayer of petition in the real sense is a presentation of our deepest needs and desires, as we understand them, to God. By presenting them to him, by talking with him about them, we eventually begin to understand how he has made us, and what is in his mind for us.

Sometimes you can trip over words when talking about petition. You recognize the difference between "needs" and "wants." Needs are those things which sustain us physically, emotionally, and spiritually. Wants can be window dressing. There is nothing wrong with them per se, but you surely recognize the difference between praying for shelter or food or employment and praying for a sports car or a box of chocolates. "Desire" is a funny word, because it crosses both categories in a way, and it depends on how you understand it. The way Saint Ignatius of Loyola speaks about it—the "desire of your heart"—is more like a need. For him desire means that which will fulfill you, make you whole, contribute to and complete your very life and personality. More ordinarily, however, desire is a want; it describes a craving or a longing. So there is something to be said for the fact that our deepest need is to let go of all desire, even the desire to be with God, as Saint John of the Cross has written. This is because our very lives are such gratuitous examples of God's deep and caring love that we must intuitively and very deeply understand that everything we are and have depends on God and on God alone, and every small detail of our lives must be lived in light of his will, not ours. So the letting go of desire in this sense—desire as a want—is really the letting go of self-will, and growth to a dependence on the single petition that makes sense: your will, Lord, not mine.

If we are truly turned to God in all we say and do, our needs will become self-evident, and if we trust God to provide for us, we will have defeated the enemy of the prayer of petition: anxiety. God knows what we need and when we need it, and he will provide insofar as we are asking for what is able to fulfill his will in our lives, which is often no more complicated than simply being and becoming who he calls us to be.

Thanksgiving

If we can learn this dependence on God's will, we find we are more often than not engaged in prayer of "thanksgiving." Again, the divisions are a little arbitrary: adoration (or praise), contrition, petition, and thanksgiving. What I mean by arbitrary is that I think they cannot exist one without the other, and each exists within the other, so that they are really all inseparable and what we mean by prayer is all four. But since they are distinct inner movements of the soul, or at least because they can be identified as such, we divide the act of praying among them. In that sense, thanksgiving brings the adoration (or praise), contrition, and petition full circle, and completes the concept of prayer.

When you think of it, it is impossible to stand before God without saying thank you in one way or another. The fact of our existence, of our consciousness, of our free will, of our intelligence, of our affections, of our very life, is so magnificent that the automatic response before the Lord is a sigh of deepest gratitude. It is on him, after all, that we depend for our very breath. And we depend on God for this and for so much more, and we thank him, constantly, as we realize that utter dependence.

There is a silly little joke that may explain what I mean. Two goldfish, swimming in a small bowl, are having a philosophical discussion. One finally says to the other: "If there's no God, who puts the food in here?" Of course, from our vantage point, we might think the pesky philosopher is wrong. But is he? We can suspect that a human is his caretaker, but is this human not in God's plan of action? The point of the story is that there are things which are beyond our very understanding, but which drive us to assume things, just the same. So the fish knows but one thing: he is somehow dependent on another being, a being beyond his own understanding, and he calls this being "God."

If we see the same sort of dependence in our own lives, we cannot help but say thank you, and say it profusely and honestly and often. But thank you for what? What do we mean when we give thanks to the Lord? At first we are tempted to say for our very lives, and this is of course true. In prayer, however, we often learn that it is more than our mere existence that drives us to such profuse gratitude. I think more often we are thanking God for his presence, not only to us deeply and personally, but among us, as the guiding force of our own lives and of those around us. Thank you becomes the word breathed in and out when God has rescued us from a bad choice or decision. Thank you is the single thought when we finally recognize, perhaps with some embarrassment, that the fault we managed to find so well in others sits squarely in the midst of our lives as well. Thank you will be the automatic reaction when what we have hoped for for so long comes to fruition and flowers in our inner lives or in our outer lives or in both.

Thanking God also involves thanking him for who we are. It is important, as you know, to like yourself. There are too many people wandering around who, in one way or another, will tell you that God in his creation of them has somehow made a mistake. Their noses are too short, or too long; their feet are too big, or too small; they are too fat, or too thin; and you know the rest. They have a litany of God's mistakes in their lives: their parents, their friends, their schooling, their neighborhood. Somehow they can manage to tell you everything that is wrong with them with just a glance. They just plain do not like themselves. They need to be like someone else, as if God painted their part of the field the wrong shade. Life would be dreary enough if all the flowers on the road were the same color; the problem with some people is that they cannot even see that they are one of the blooms.

Sometimes this can be very serious, but many times it is just a stage through which we all must muddle. There will be days or months or years when nothing you do seems right. And in these days and months and years you will wonder what, exactly, you have to be thankful for. I mean you will have much more to contend with than the failed examination or the missed train. The rain that falls on your parade might be accompanied by thunder or lightning or hailstones or violent wind. The hurricane that might rage inside your life could threaten to uproot your very soul. From that vantage point it can become very difficult to find something to thank the Lord about. About the only thing I can say is that no storm lasts forever. God, somehow, is in its eye, and will guide you as he guides everything else. Sometimes when we pray, we are praying to change God's will rather than to accept it. It might be well to look at how the word "*fiat*" includes the deepest thanks for who we are, and who we may become, even if we do not know quite yet what exactly that might be. *Fiat*, you recall, is the single word that summarizes Mary's answer to the angel's announcement that she would become the mother of Jesus, the Son of God. *Fiat* means "Let it be." Let it happen. Yes. I agree. Yes.

When you think of it, that is a pretty difficult concept. God asked Mary, a young woman a little younger than yourself, to bear his Son. He asked her to live a confusing life, to have a child whose name had been promised in Scripture, but whose presence would confound the pious. She had to have been frightened, but the part of her heart reserved for its deepest intuitions, the place within her kept silent to hear God's word, immediately told her yes, this is right, and so she said in full voice "*Fiat*." She said yes to what was real in her life.

This is the healthiest prayer we can utter. I was told by a wise woman once that holiness means simply dealing with reality. I hope that never leaves me, and I give it here as perhaps the best words I can pass along to you. Dreams have no hard surfaces against which we skin our knees, and lots of people need to escape into them. Reality, in life and in prayer, is where we find our holiness and our trust in God tested daily and often and well. When thanksgiving becomes a real *fiat* to all we are and have, and all we will become in God's care, we are moving toward the kind of peace that holiness brings.

I wish I could be more specific. I have met holy people. One I think of now is perhaps indicative of the rest. She lives where she is. Not where she has been, or where she will be, or even where she might like to be. She is present, absolutely present, where and when she is where she is. That means she focuses her entire attention on those with whom she speaks. Her mind is not listening for the doorbell or thinking about dinner. That absolute attention goes to you, or to me, or to God. I think she is constantly grateful for what God brings her, no matter who or what, and I have a sense about her that she might have a special private line into the heavenly choirs. So convinced is she of God's action in the world and in individuals' lives, she is always saying "thank you."

I think that is a good practice. Thanking God, for who we are and who we will be, is an act both of gratitude and of profound obeisance, for embedded in the thanks is the renunciation of will that leads us to additional thanks, and back to adoration of the God who so very tenderly cares for us and understands our every move and motive.

Methods of Prayer

T hese four "breaths," if you will, of prayer—adoration or praise, contrition, petition, and thanksgiving—can fit into a number of different methods of praying. No one method is better or worse than any other, so long as it brings you to God.

I have spent a lot of time telling you what not to do, and being rather clinical in dividing up the single breath of prayer. Now it might be well to tell you more about how to meet the call to prayer within you. I sometimes think there is an internal shofar that calls us all to prayer at regular intervals, and that the more we ignore it, the more we find ourselves uneasy. Prayer itself is not always easy, but I think if you begin to be a little sensitive to your needs for quiet and for resting in the peaceful presence of the Lord, you will indeed find that little horn sounding regularly. Do not think of it as a warning or a factory whistle calling you to a specific task. Try more to think of it as a foghorn, calling you forth when perhaps you have lost your way, or as the dismissal bell, allowing you to drop whatever task you have set before you for the day, to move into the recreation and the re-creation of prayer.

Many writers speak of the four steps of prayer as *lectio* (reading), *meditatio* (meditation), *oratio* (speaking), and *contemplatio* (contemplation). This is another way of recalling the movements of your heart, for you most commonly will take a Scripture passage and read it, then apply your mind's eye to it, then speak with the Lord about the ways in which it applies to your life and ask for what you need, and, finally, rest in God's comfort and love as you receive his reply. This is a good way of organizing your thoughts about prayer, of understanding the movements of your soul. In the larger sense, it is also a good way to organize your day with God: some reading of or about his word, some mental application of the word to your situation, some genuine conversation with the Lord, and some resting in his love. This is a monastic, or Benedictine, approach, and if it suits you I would urge you to follow it.

These steps more generally help prepare every soul for an encounter with the Lord. Each is a part of preparing the soul as if it were God's garden: turning over the soil and feeding it with reading, watering it and giving it sun with meditation, attending to it with concern and care in conversation with God, and receiving God's breath of life with contemplation.

But just as it is not necessary to clinically divide all of your life with God into one or another "breath" of adoration (or praise), petition, contrition, or thanksgiving, it is not necessary to be that involved with the divisions of *lectio, meditatio, oratio,* or *contemplatio,* except insofar as you know about them and recognize that each will help you along the way.

Meditation

U sed more generally, meditation is a word that covers most kinds of prayer we ordinarily do alone. It involves the mind, as the mind touches the heart, and the heart moves toward God. But it is more than just sitting around thinking gooey thoughts, and trying by those gooey thoughts to elicit some equally gooey feelings about God. Meditation, I think, means getting involved in what we know as conversation with God, and testing our own feelings as either he or we present specific things, or as specific things come to mind. It will include all four movements we spoke of above: adoration or praise, contrition, petition, and thanksgiving.

Sometimes meditation is lightning fast: we decide to meditate upon a crucifix, or perhaps upon a painting of a saint. Suddenly, we find ourselves engaged in deep, honest conversation with the Lord. Or, suddenly, we feel he is speaking directly to us. This flash of intuition is unmistakable, and real. There are many stories of saints who found crucifixes "speaking" to them: Saint Thomas Aquinas knelt before a crucifix in the Dominican church in Naples and found the Lord speaking to him quite deeply; Saint Francis of Assisi had a similar experience at the church of San Damiano, just outside his hometown. These two come to mind, but I am sure there are more. Do not be too surprised if a crucifix "speaks" to your heart some day. Of course I do not mean you will be able to videotape the conversation, but there may be times when God is so close and so real that he genuinely "speaks" to you, and startles you a bit at that.

So when you meditate, then, what will you do? I can recall being in Rome on a Saturday afternoon some years ago, needing to forgive some people who I thought had hurt me deeply. The hurt was real, and I could not understand why, if I had done what I knew I was supposed to do, I seemed to lose so much. I happened on a church that has a huge and very life-like crucifix, and I knelt. Before I knew it, words were moving so fast through my mind I could not count them, and the impression that flashed across my heart brought forth an incredible compassion for the Christ before me. Somehow I began, just a little, to understand his passion, his frailty, his humanity. More so, I began to know that he really did know how I felt, what I was feeling. I can recall knowing in my deepest soul that my own upset and loss and embarrassment were shared in a very human way by the man represented in plaster before me, whose life story, told a thousand times, is the granite base of my own belief, and of my self-understanding.

Was this a meditation? I do not know. I cannot recall the precise details of the time I spent that day. The people who write about prayer often say that every meditation has "points" through which one moves, a sort of recipe or road map to help you out. These instructions cannot be ignored. Only the foolhardy will try to go down the expert "black diamond" slope at a ski resort the first day out. So the instructions are for beginners. The thing about it is we are all beginners at various times in our lives, and so the instructions are for all of us who every so often have to begin all over again.

Basically, before we come to our time for prayer, we will have found something to start us off. It is often best to decide before your prayer time what you will use, because it is too easy to spend twenty or thirty minutes or so just leafing through Scripture, or paging through a picture book, and before you know it your prayer time has evaporated into a hurried ten minutes or so that doesn't really go anyplace. Many people very regularly use a scene or a passage from Scripture to bring them into deep conversation with the Lord. Sometimes, if you have been discussing your interior life with a spiritual guide or director, he or she may suggest that you pay particular attention to certain moments in our Lord's life. Or you may be the methodological type, and work your own way through book after book of the Bible when nothing else seems to strike your heart. Or sometimes you will be so filled with this wonderful relationship that just about anything at all, a newspaper article, a postcard from a friend, a line in a book, will launch you into the most prayerful conversation with God.

In any event, with whatever you use, there is a formula you can follow. For example, you may read a small passage of Scripture, slowly, and ask God for the grace you need. This grace may be something that has been suggested to you, such as the grace to see God's hand in all you do, or the grace to better understand the mystery of Eucharist, or the grace of forgiveness for a particular hurt. Then, as you go back over the passage, you will find there are things which strike you especially, "points" on which you can expand, things that help you better talk with God about your needs. I cannot tell you what they are, and I hesitate even to give you an example. You may go your whole lifelong without ever needing to pray for some of the things I beg God for daily, and there is no sense in thinking yourself odd if it never occurs to you to ask God to give you what I am begging for myself. We are different people, and he knows that better than anyone.

As you talk with God, you will understand what gift he has for you. As the result of your prayer, you might find a single word or phrase that will bring you back to this wonderful conversation during the day. It might be simply "I love you," or "Dear Lord, where are you?" or "God, help me keep my tongue," but the Lord will prompt you. It is as simple and as difficult as that.

Praying With Scripture

~

There are many ways by which we enter into meditative prayer. One of the easiest is to take a scene from the gospel and imagine it. This is a way taught by Saint Ignatius of Loyola. If you read a passage where Jesus is doing or saying something, you can imagine yourself right there, in the middle of the crowd watching, or you can imagine yourself as the person to whom he speaks. What would you do? What would you say to Jesus in this instant? Can you imagine the scene, really imagine it—the sounds and the smells and the feelings it all brings up to you? If you let yourself be drawn into a particular passage of Scripture, you will find yourself saying things to Jesus, or noticing that the things he says and does touch you very deeply in your most private history. You will notice how you feel when Jesus says or does a particular thing, and how you feel when you respond to his word or to his touch.

Let me give you just one example. There is a passage in the Gospel of Saint John that describes the way in which the crowds disagreed about Jesus, as to whether or not he was the Messiah. The chief priests and the Pharisees are arguing about Jesus, and they complain that the guards have not arrested him, as they were ordered to. The passage continues:

The guards went back to the chief priests and Pharisees who said to them, "Why haven't you brought him?" The guards replied. "No one has ever spoken like this man." "So," the Pharisees answered, "you, too, have been led astray? Have any of the authorities come to believe in him? Any of the Pharisees? This rabble knows nothing about the Law—they are damned." One of them, Nicodemus—the same man who had come to Jesus earlier—said to them, "But surely our Law does not allow us to pass judgment on anyone without first giving him a hearing and discovering what he is doing?" To this they answered, "Are you a Galilean too? Go into the matter, and see for yourself: prophets do not arise in Galilee" (John 7:45–52).

Now, as you read this, certain thoughts may come to mind. These are the things you might talk about with God, the "points" for your meditation. For example, maybe a friend has stood up for you in a very painful situation, where you could not speak for yourself. Or perhaps you have been in a situation where you were ignored just because of who you were, or where you were from, or what you were wearing, or the manner in which you speak. Many other people have these same experiences, but none has them exactly as you do, so it is important for you to discuss the matter with God. How that works, exactly, is a mystery. But we place ourselves in God's presence, as we understand it, and simply read the passage over a few times, stopping when something touches us in our hearts. This is what we speak about to God. We tell him how we feel, perhaps about being rejected. We thank him for the friend or friends who stood up for us. We have to be very careful not to criticize those who have hurt us—the chief priests and Pharisees of our own lives—because that can start a bitterness that is very hard to uproot. It is, in fact, a little presumptuous even to pray for their conversion, because it is important to remember that people, for the most part, are acting in good faith and are acting in accord with their own circumstances and consciences. Yet perhaps the frustration and humiliation we suffer is the frustration and humiliation of not being heard, and so these chief priests and Pharisees who judge us can be accused of not listening. This is a big accusation, and we need to listen to God as he speaks to us about this. Maybe their not listening is an indication that they are not worthy of judging us; justice, after all, implies treating those judged with dignity and respect. We do not need to tell God what he already knows, but it is always a big help to just throw all our troubles at him in the hope he will respond.

As you begin your meditation, all kinds of thoughts and feelings may come to you, and you are anxious to rush off and tell God everything, because you are afraid you might forget something. This is normal and sometimes gets us confused. The way to gain some security is to recall that God knows all we want to say before we say it, and we need only to say it to understand how we feel about it. That is why we need to pay attention to our feelings in prayer. We also need to pay attention to what it is we think we need—what we find ourselves asking for in prayer. Sometimes we ask for something to happen: for a friend, like Nicodemus to defend us when or where we cannot speak. Sometimes we ask for those who stand for justice, those chief priests and Pharisees, to give us a little of the justice they claim to give to those who need it most. Sometimes we ask for a memory to be healed, for God to show us how it all makes sense in our life. And sometimes we ask just to be consoled, for God to do nothing more than to make us feel a little better about whatever it is that has hurt us so deeply—the rejection we feel, just like Jesus, because of where we are from (Galilee?), or how we speak, or what we stand for. Or perhaps we need to apologize for not being who we really can be, for not standing up for someone else and defending him or her.

I cannot tell you exactly what will happen, or what you may or may not say, when you talk with God about this passage. And I certainly cannot tell you what God will say, or how he will speak to you in your heart about this section of Scripture. Maybe you will have nothing to say. And maybe God will have nothing to say. So you will pass right over these pages and latch on to something else that speaks more deeply to you. Then, perhaps a year or ten years from now, something in this particular passage will strike you and you will find that you have spent forty-five minutes or an hour in deep and peaceful communication with the God who touches you most deeply, and you will learn from him how better to live your life in his service in a way that I really cannot explain to you now, or ever.

Contemplation

Sometimes when you are praying like this you will notice that a particular quiet fastens itself around you, and you have an extraordinary understanding of the love of God. The Lord, in fact, is often quite lavish in his response to people who are just beginning to regularize their lives of prayer, whether for the first or for the fourteenth time. This special quiet in God's care can be a movement toward what is known as contemplative prayer. This is not unlike the movement or stage of adoration I spoke of earlier, yet it is the way in which adoration and praise, contrition, petition, and thanksgiving are expressed wordlessly.

There are many movements within contemplative prayer and, even at the beginning, some unusual things may occur. I do not want to put ideas in your head but, if anything extraordinary occurs when you find yourself praying like this, you might want to examine your own reactions as a test of their validity. I guess the best thing I can tell you is that if you are afraid *while* some things are happening, then you probably have the right reaction, that is, they are like as not to be examples of a bad digestion as of anything else, but they are probably not from God. If, however, you find yourself recalling extraordinary feelings or events after your prayer, but know that during prayer you were not in the least afraid, then these things quite probably came from God. It is important not to look for anything, and to trust that God will either explain your experience or provide you with someone who can gently explain his ways.

It is said that Pascal wrote, on a very small piece of paper that he kept with him his whole life, a sentence which merely said: "The light, the incredible light." I cannot tell you how God will manifest himself to you, or how or when he will draw you deeper into an extended wordless communion of his love. I can promise you, however, that as you work at prayer and prayerfulness you will find his presence much more real and frequent, and your own relationship will be much less one of "Hello, Mr. God" and more the easy presence of a friend and possibly the passionate embrace of the lover who wordlessly explains to you the totality of your being.

All ways of praying, all "breaths" of prayer, can move you to contemplation. Simple adoration is not quite the same as contemplation, but it can lead to it. As you move along in your life of prayer, no doubt you will find others who have written about it much more expertly than I am able to do. Spiritual writers clearly describe the movement toward contemplation for us. Saint Teresa of Ávila, the sixteenth-century Carmelite reformer and Doctor of the Church, says there are seven stages in the spiritual life, seven crystal mansions filled with many rooms through which the soul progresses on her way to meet the King at the center. To move to real contemplation, she tells us, we begin in the first three mansions with simple meditation, the kind of praying with Scripture or paintings or memories I described above, accompanied by pious reading and the practice of charity. These ready us for the gift of the fourth mansion: the prayer of quiet. Here, she tells us, God invites the soul to a contemplative life with him, a gift continued in the fifth and sixth mansions.

This prayer of quiet is much talked about and much misunderstood and I hesitate to go beyond my depth. Let me simply say that its mark, aside from an absolute receptive quiet in the soul, is a gradual letting go of even the least ounce of self-will. It is the absolute peace of giving up all control to a wordless trusting in God. There is no preference, one way or the other, for anything, even for the knowledge of the presence of God.

You recall I told you that some writers say we must let go of all desire, even the desire for God, in order to progress in the spiritual life. This may seem contradictory but if you think of it a bit it does make sense. The complete dependence upon God removes all desire from our soul, so that the only desire extant is that God's will will come about, either within the moment of prayer (and so he will manifest himself or not, as he chooses) or within the context of our exterior lives (and so he will grant a "desire" or not).

Within the smaller moment, I believe it is during this time of prayer that God makes his will best known to us, often inviting us to do the most startling (and apparently impossible) things. A trap here is known as "quietism," which is a misunderstanding of how we are to be in God's hands. Obviously, we bring our whole lives and understandings to the fore when we talk with God, or rest in his presence. But without guidance in the prayer of quiet we can very easily turn into unanchored buoys bobbing in the channel, turning round and round with each change of the tide, and eventually just floating undirected out to sea.

So it is good to listen to the spiritual writers, as well as the personal guides we find. Teresa is an interesting woman, and she gently tells us that contemplative prayer must be grounded in meditation. Her fourth, fifth, and sixth mansions describe what is known as infused contemplation, and in speaking about the sixth mansion she describes a deep intuitive meditation on and an understanding of the humanity of Christ. This is very important, and central to all our ways and methods of praying: Christ is at the center of all prayer because Christ is at the center of all humanity. Saint Teresa teaches us that once passed through this sixth mansion, the soul moves to the seventh mansion and the mystical marriage with Christ. This seventh mansion, at the center of the spiritual life, is what other women— such as another woman Doctor of the Church, Saint Catherine of Siena—describe so vividly and so well. Here the realm of mysticism takes over; it is a level few reach and none can achieve. This is a wholly gratuitous gift of God.

Contemplative prayer has these many stages. On the one hand, it is the Olympic level of prayer. On the other, it is the simplest. Not everyone is called to contemplation all the time, but it is not inconceivable that all can find themselves lost in it some of the time. It is, as I have said, the type of prayer that is at once most glorious and most dangerous, because of the ever-present specter of solipsism. There are many other states especially which can masquerade as the fourth mansion, and most people who seriously attempt prayer of this sort seek some advice from another more experienced, the spiritual guide or director I mentioned earlier, just as a matter of checks and balances.

However dull or even threatening that might seem, we really do need to talk with others about our lives with God. This may be very hard for you, especially if your natural shyness extends to what is really your most private relationship. It is, I know, quite hard to learn to talk about your prayer life. As hard as it is to talk about prayer, it is also rather hard to listen to. By that I mean, there are many people around who hold themselves out as spiritual guides or directors, but as soon as you begin to describe the ways in which you experience God, they change the subject, or cough, or somehow signal (even unconsciously) that they do not want to hear about it. This can be awfully frustrating, but it has happened to me at the very worst times, and it may well happen to you.

I would not be afraid or upset about this. In fact, it is entirely possible that God is not providing someone to talk with about prayer because there is nothing to talk about, or because you really want to talk with someone other than God about your troubles and God would prefer you talk with him. I promise you that if you need a good spiritual director, one will appear somehow. I would urge you to be conscious of whether you need one or not, especially when things are going on in your prayer that you do not understand, and very especially if there is something inside you which is urging you in a rather indigestive way not to discuss your interior life with anyone at all. That to me is the surest sign of the need for direction.

In Conclusion

N ow that you are twenty-one even I, your poor godmother, must adopt a "hands off" attitude toward your relations with God and with the Church. So I am glad we talked about prayer when we did. It was, after all, my last chance to legitimately bring the subject up on my own. When I began to think about our conversation after your birthday party, and how I might tell you about prayer, I thought I might just give you psalms to pray, without any introduction or comment. I planned just to choose some psalms and some photographs from newspapers, and tell you to place yourself in God's presence and talk with him about them. In a way, I guess I am still doing that. I do not mean to overburden you with details with my introduction to this little book—workbook, if you will—of psalms and Scripture passages that I hope will bring you to a deeper relationship with God. That is all I mean to do, to point you toward the Lord and his people, to encourage you in a life of prayer and service, which will both cause and be caused by a deeper relationship with God.

These are some psalms and parts of psalms and some passages from Scripture that have moved my heart and I hope will move yours. The psalms are in no particular order, except numerical. They are just bits and pieces of the one hundred fifty psalms of David, which the Church uses to celebrate the liturgical hours every day. The passages are ones you may know already. I cannot say I mean each one specifically for you at this very moment, but they are sufficiently broad that I think you can use one or another of them. I just thought they might be useful as aids to prayer.

That is, after all, what it is all about. I can write all I want, and you and I can talk forever, but the bottom line of it all is prayer. Sometimes that is hard work, and you feel as if you are walking in a desert, or, worse, a desert storm. This "dryness," as it is called, can be discouraging but it does not last forever. I promise you that after a while you will come upon a little spring that will turn into a stream. Then the depth and breadth of it all will amaze you, and you will lose yourself in God's love as easily as you slip off to sleep.

There is not much more I can say. Or, better, there is not much more I should say. I do not mean that you and I can never talk about this beautiful part of our lives. I simply mean that my words can only bring you to the edge, and that from here you are on your own.

The wonderful thing, of course, is that you are on your own with God. I commend you, therefore, to his care, because I love you.

Scripture Passages

1 Samuel 3:1–9
God Calls Samuel

Now, the boy Samuel was serving Yahweh in the presence of Eli; in those days it was rare for Yahweh to speak; visions were uncommon. One day, it happened that Eli was lying down in his room. His eyes were beginning to grow dim; he could no longer see. The lamp of God had not yet gone out, and Samuel was lying in Yahweh's sanctuary, where the ark of God was, when Yahweh called, "Samuel! Samuel!" He answered, "Here I am," and, running to Eli, he said, "Here I am, as you called me." Eli said, "I did not call. Go back and lie down." So he went and lay down. And again Yahweh called, "Samuel! Samuel!" He got up and went to Eli and said, "Here I am, as you called me." He replied, "I did not call you, my son; go back and lie down." Samuel had as yet no knowledge of Yahweh and the word of Yahweh had not yet been revealed to him. Once again

Yahweh called, the third time. He got up and went to Eli and said, "Here I am, since you called me." Eli then understood that Yahweh was calling the child, and he said to Samuel, "Go and lie down, and if someone calls say, 'Speak, Yahweh; for your servant is listening.'" So Samuel went and lay down in his place.

Psalm 1
The Two Paths

Happy indeed is the one
who follows not the counsel of the wicked;
nor lingers in the way of sinners
nor sits in the company of scorners,
but whose delight is the law of the Lord
and who ponders his law day and night.

He is like a tree that is planted
beside the flowing waters,
that yields its fruit in due season
and whose leaves shall never fade;
and all that he does shall prosper.
Not so are the wicked, not so!

For they like winnowed chaff
shall be driven away by the wind.
When the wicked are judged they shall not stand,
nor find room among those who are just;
do not envy those who do evil:
for the Lord guards the way of the just
but the way of the wicked leads to doom.

Psalm 37
The Lot of the Wicked and the Good

Do not fret because of the wicked;
do not envy those who do evil:
for they wither quickly like grass
and fade like the green of the fields.

If you trust in the Lord and do good,
then you will live in the land and be secure.
If you find your delight in the Lord,
he will grant your heart's desire.

Commit your life to the Lord,
trust in him and he will act,
so that your justice breaks forth like the light,
your cause like the noon-day sun.

Be still before the Lord and wait in patience;
do not fret at the man who prospers;
a man who makes evil plots
to bring down the needy and the poor.

Calm your anger and forget your rage;
do not fret, it only leads to evil.
For those who do evil shall perish;
the patient shall inherit the land.

A little longer—and the wicked shall have gone.
Look at his place, he is not there.
But the humble shall own the land
and enjoy the fullness of peace

Psalm 139:1–10, 13–14
God Sees All That Is

O Lord, you search me and you know me,
you know my resting and my rising,
you discern my purpose from afar.
You mark when I walk or lie down,
all my ways lie open to you.

Before ever a word is on my tongue
you know it, O Lord, through and through.
Behind and before you besiege me,
your hand ever laid upon me.
Too wonderful for me, this knowledge,
too high, beyond my reach.

O where can I go from your spirit
or where can I flee from your face?
If I climb the heavens, you are there.
If I lie in the grave, you are there.

If I take the winds of the dawn
and dwell at the sea's furthest end,
even there your hand would lead me,
your right hand would hold me fast.

For it was you who created my being,
knit me together in my mother's womb.
I thank you for the wonder of my being,
for the wonders of all your creation.

Matthew 22:34–40
The Greatest
Commandment of All

But when the Pharisees heard that he had silenced the Sadducees they got together and, to put him to the test, one of them put a further question, "Master, which is the greatest commandment of the Law?" Jesus said to him, "You must love the Lord your God with all your heart, with all your soul, and with all your mind. This is the greatest and the first commandment. The second resembles it: You must love your neighbor as yourself. On these two commandments hang the whole Law, and the Prophets too."

Isaiah 58:1-12
Fasting Is Pleasing to God

Shout for all you are worth, do not hold back,
   raise your voice like a trumpet.
To my people proclaim their rebellious acts,
   to the House of Jacob, their sins.
They seek for me day after day,
   they long to know my ways,
   like a nation that has acted uprightly
   and not forsaken the law of its God.
They ask me for laws that are upright,
   they long to be near God:
"Why have we fasted, if you do not see,
   why mortify ourselves if you never notice?"
Look, you seek your own pleasure on your fast days
   and you exploit all your workmen;
   look, the only purpose of your fasting is to
   quarrel and squabble
   and strike viciously with your fist.
Fasting like yours today
   will never make your voice heard on high.
Is that the sort of fast that pleases me,
   a day when a person inflicts pain on himself?

Hanging your head like a reed,
*   spreading out sackcloth and ashes?*
Is that what you call fasting,
*   a day acceptable to Yahweh?*
Is not this the sort of fast that pleases me:
*   to break unjust fetters,*
*   to undo the thongs of the yoke,*
*   to let the oppressed go free,*
*   and to break all yokes?*
Is it not sharing your food with the hungry,
*   and sheltering the homeless poor;*
*   if you see someone lacking clothes, to clothe him,*
*   and not turn away from your own kin?*
Then your light will blaze out like the dawn
*   and your wound will be quickly healed over.*
Saving justice for you will go ahead
*   and Yahweh's glory come behind you.*
Then you will cry for help and Yahweh will answer;
*   and you will call and he will say, "I am here."*
If you do away with the yoke,
*   the clenched fist and malicious words,*
*   if you deprive yourself for the hungry*
*   your light will rise in the darkness,*
*   and your darkest hour will be like noon.*
Yahweh will always guide you,
*   will satisfy your needs in the scorched land;*

> *he will give strength to your bones*
> *and you will be like a watered garden,*
> *like a flowing spring*
> *whose waters never run dry.*
> *Your ancient ruins will be rebuilt;*
> *you will build on age-old foundations.*
> *You will be called "Breach-mender,"*
> *"Restorer of streets to be lived in."*

Jeremiah 18:1–6
Jeremiah Visits the Potter

The word that came to Jeremiah from Yahweh as follows, "Get up and make your way down to the potter's house, and there I shall tell you what I have to say." So I went down to the potter's house; and there he was, working at the wheel. But the vessel he was making came out wrong, as may happen with clay when a potter is at work. So he began again and shaped it into another vessel, as he thought fit. The word of Yahweh came to me as follows, "House of Israel, can I not do to you what this potter does?" Yahweh demands. "Yes, like clay in the potter's hand, so you are in mine, House of Israel."

Hosea 2:16, 2–22
Yahweh and His Wife

That is why I am going to lure her and lead her out into the wilderness and speak to her heart....

I will betroth you to myself forever, betroth you with integrity and justice, with tenderness and love.

I will betroth you to myself with faithfulness, and you will come to know Yahweh.

Ecclesiastics 27:4-8
On Speech

In a shaken sieve the rubbish is left behind,
*   so too the defects of a person appear in speech.*
The kiln tests the work of the potter,
*   the test of a person is in conversation.*
The orchard where the tree grows is judged
*   by its fruit;*
*   similarly words betray what a person feels.*
Do not praise anyone who has not yet spoken,
*   since this is where people are tested.*

Mark 4:35–41
The Calming of the Storm

With the coming of evening that same day, he said to them, "Let us cross over to the other side." And leaving the crowd behind they took him, just as he was, in the boat; and there were other boats with him. Then it began to blow a great gale and the waves were breaking into the boat so that it was almost swamped. But he was in the stern, his head on the cushion, asleep. They woke him and said to him, "Master, do you not care? We are lost!" And he woke up and rebuked the wind and said to the sea, "Quiet now! Be calm!" And the wind dropped, and there followed a great calm. Then he said to them, "Why are you so frightened? Have you still no faith?" They were overcome with awe and said to one another, "Who can this be? Even the wind and the sea obey him."

Mark 5:25-3
Cure of the Woman With a Hemorrhage

Now there was a woman who had suffered a hemorrhage for twelve years; after long and painful treatment under various doctors, she had spent all she had without being any the better for it; in fact, she was getting worse. She had heard about Jesus, and she came up through the crowd and touched his cloak from behind, thinking, "If I can just touch his clothes, I shall be saved." And at once the source of the bleeding dried up, and she felt herself that she was cured of her complaint. And at once aware of the power that had gone out from him, Jesus turned round in the crowd and said, "Who touched my clothes?" His disciples said to him, "You see how the crowd is pressing round you; how can you ask, 'Who touched me?'" But he continued to look all round to see who had done it. Then the woman came forward, frightened and trembling because she knew what had happened to her, and she fell at his feet and told him the whole truth. "My daughter," he said, your faith has restored you to health; go in peace and be free of your complaint."

Luke 1:26–38
The Annunciation

In the sixth month the angel Gabriel was sent by God to a town in Galilee called Nazareth, to a virgin betrothed to a man named Joseph, of the House of David; and the virgin's name was Mary. He went in and said to her, "Rejoice, you who enjoy God's favor. Look! You are to conceive in your womb and bear a son, and you must name him Jesus. He will be great and will be called Son of the Most High. The Lord God will give him the throne of his ancestor David; he will rule over the House of Jacob for ever and his reign will have no end." Mary said to the angel, "But how can this come about since I have no knowledge of man?" The angel answered, "The Holy Spirit will come upon you, and the power of the Most High will cover you with its shadow. And so the child will be holy and will be called Son of God. And I tell you this too: your cousin Elizabeth also, in her old age, has conceived a son, and she whom people called barren is now in her sixth month, for nothing is impossible with God." Mary said, "You see before you the Lord's servant, let it happen to me as you have said." And the angel left her.

John 4:46–53
The Cure
of the Royal Official's Son

Jesus went again to Cana in Galilee, where he had changed the water into wine. And there was a court official whose son was ill at Capernaum; hearing that Jesus had arrived in Galilee from Judaea he went and asked him to come and cure his son, as he was at the point of death. Jesus said to him, "Unless you see signs and portents you will not believe!" "Sir," answered the official, "come down before my child dies." "Go home," said Jesus, "your son will live." The man believed what Jesus had said and went on his way home; and while he was still on the way his servants met him with the news that his boy was alive. He asked them when the boy had begun to recover. They replied, "The fever left him yesterday at the seventh hour." The father realized that this was exactly the time when Jesus had said, "Your son will live"; and he and all his household believed.

Acts 10:34–43
Peter's Address at the House of Cornelius

Then Peter addressed them: "I now really understand," he said, "that God has no favorites, but that anybody of any nationality who fears him and does what is right is acceptable to him.

"God sent his word to the people of Israel, and it was to them that the good news of peace was brought by Jesus Christ—he is the Lord of all. You know what happened all over Judaea, how Jesus of Nazareth began in Galilee, after John had been preaching baptism. God had anointed him with the Holy Spirit and with power, and because God was with him, Jesus went about doing good and curing all who had fallen into the power of the devil. Now we are witnesses to everything he did throughout the countryside of Judaea and in Jerusalem itself: and they killed him by hanging him on a tree, yet on the third day God raised him to life and allowed him to be seen, not by the whole people but only by certain witnesses that God had chosen beforehand. Now we are those witnesses—we have eaten and drunk with him after his resurrection from the dead— and he has ordered us to proclaim this to his people and to bear witness that God has appointed him to judge everyone, alive or dead. It is to him that all the prophets bear this witness: that all who believe in Jesus will have their sins forgiven through his name."

Romans 12:12–19
Spiritual Worship

Be joyful in hope, persevere in hardship; keep praying regularly; share with any of God's holy people who are in need; look for opportunities to be hospitable.

Bless your persecutors; never curse them; bless them. Rejoice with others when they rejoice, and be sad with those in sorrow. Give the same consideration to all others alike. Pay no regard to social standing, but meet humble people on their own terms. Do not congratulate yourself on your own wisdom. Never pay back evil with evil, but bear in mind the ideals that all regard with respect. As much as possible, and to the utmost of your ability, be at peace with everyone. Never try to get revenge.

Galatians 5:13–26
Liberty and Love

After all, you were called to be free; do not use your freedom as an opening for self-indulgence, but be servants to one another in love, since the whole of the Law is summarized in the one commandment: You must love your neighbor as yourself. If you go snapping at one another and tearing one another to pieces, take care: you will be eaten up by one another.

Instead, I tell you, be guided by the Spirit, and you will no longer yield to self-indulgence. The desires of self-indulgence are always in opposition to the Spirit, and the desires of the Spirit are in opposition to self-indulgence: they are opposites, one against the other; that is how you are prevented from doing the things that you want to. But when you are led by the Spirit, you are not under the Law. When self-indulgence is at work the results are obvious: sexual vice, impurity, and sensuality, the worship of false gods and sorcery; antagonisms and rivalry, jealousy, bad temper and quarrels, disagreements, factions and malice, drunkenness, orgies and all such things. And about these, I tell you now as I have told you in the past, that people who behave in these ways will not inherit the kingdom of

God. On the other hand the fruit of the Spirit is love, joy, peace, patience, kindness, goodness, trustfulness, gentleness and self-control; no law can touch such things as these. All who belong to Christ Jesus have crucified self with all its passions and desires.

Since we are living by the Spirit, let our behavior be guided by the Spirit and let us not be conceited or provocative and envious of one another.

Ephesians 6:10–20
The Spiritual War

Finally, grow strong in the Lord, with the strength of his power. Put on the full armor of God so as to be able to resist the devil's tactics. For it is not against human enemies that we have to struggle, but against the principalities and the ruling forces who are masters of the darkness in this world, the spirits of evil in the heavens. That is why you must take up all God's armor, or you will not be able to put up any resistance on the evil day, or stand your ground even though you exert yourselves to the full.

So stand your ground, with truth a belt round your waist, and uprightness a breastplate, wearing for shoes on your feet the eagerness to spread the gospel of peace and always carrying the shield of faith so that you can use it to quench the burning arrows of the Evil One. And then you must take salvation as your helmet and the sword of the Spirit, that is, the word of God.

In all your prayer and entreaty keep praying in the Spirit on every possible occasion. Never get tired of staying awake to pray for all God's holy people, and pray for me to be given an opportunity to open my mouth and fearlessly make known the mystery of the gospel of which I am an ambassador in chains; pray that in proclaiming it I may speak as fearlessly as I ought to.

Other books on prayer from Liguori Publications

Praying With Sacred Beads
Joan Hutson

Short Prayers for the Long Day
Compiled by Giles and Melville Harcourt

Soliloquy Prayer
Unfolding Our Hearts to God
Dennis Billy, C.Ss.R.

At Prayer With the Saints
Compiled by Anthony F. Chiffolo

The Healing Power of Prayer
Bridget Mary Meehan

Centered Living
The Way of Centering Prayer
M. Basil Pennington, O.C.S.O.

Praying the Name of Jesus
The Ancient Wisdom of the Jesus Prayer
Wilfrid Stinissen